ANATOMY CLASS

Human Organs

by Kristi Lew

Consultant:
Marjorie J. Hogan, MD
Associate Professor
University of Minnesota, Minneapolis

Capstone
press®

Mankato, Minnesota

Fact Finders is published by Capstone Press,
151 Good Counsel Drive, P.O. Box 669, Mankato, Minnesota 56002.
www.capstonepress.com

Books published by Capstone Press are manufactured with paper
containing at least 10 percent post-consumer waste.

Library of Congress Cataloging-in-Publication Data
Lew, Kristi.
    Human organs / by Kristi Lew.
    p. cm. — (Fact finders. Anatomy class)
    Includes bibliographical references and index.
    Summary: "Describes the organs of the human body, including vital and non-vital
organs" — Provided by publisher.
    ISBN 978-1-4296-3339-0 (library binding)
    ISBN 978-1-4296-3886-9 (softcover)
    1. Organs (Anatomy) — Juvenile literature. I. Title. II. Series.
QM27.L49 2010
611 — dc22   2009002775

Editorial Credits
Lori Shores, editor; Ted Williams, designer; Svetlana Zhurkin, media researcher

Photo Credits
BigStockPhoto/Tracy Hornbrook, 27
Getty Images/3D4Medical, cover, 8, 15 (inset); Stock Illustration Source/Christopher Creek, 12
iStockphoto/Aaliya Landholt, 24; Agnieszka Steinhagen, 16; Sebastian Kaulitzki, 19, 23
Peter Arnold/Manfred Kage, 7 (inset)
Shutterstock/Alexandar Iotzov, 5; Sebastian Kaulitzki, 11, 15, 29
Visuals Unlimited/Dr. David Phillips, 21; Medicimage, 23 (inset); Veronika Burmeister, 7

Essential content terms are **bold** are defined at the bottom of the page where they first appear

Table of Contents

Human Organs

Lots of people work together to make life in a city possible. Some people work in bakeries and make food. Police and firefighters make sure the city is safe. And other people keep the city clean. Everyone has a job to do.

Your body is sort of like a city too. Every organ in the human body has an important job to do. Your lungs help you breathe. Your heart pumps blood through your body. And your brain controls everything. In your body, your organs work together to keep you alive.

Organs are grouped together into organ systems. For example, your stomach, small intestine, and large intestine make up your digestive system. These organs break down the food you eat for energy. The organs in each system work together to do a particular job.

Organs or Not?

Can you name your body's largest organ? Is it your brain? No. What about your heart or lungs? No, it's not either one of these. The body's largest organ isn't inside the body at all. It's on the outside. People look at and touch it every day. Skin is your body's largest organ. In fact, the average adult has between 6 and 8 pounds (2.7 and 3.6 kilograms) of skin.

Your skin covers and protects the rest of your body. It keeps your **internal** organs on the inside where they belong. Without your skin, your guts would spill out all over the place. But your skin does more than just hold you together. Skin keeps dirt and germs out of your body. It also stores water, fat, and vitamin D for the body to use.

internal — inside the body

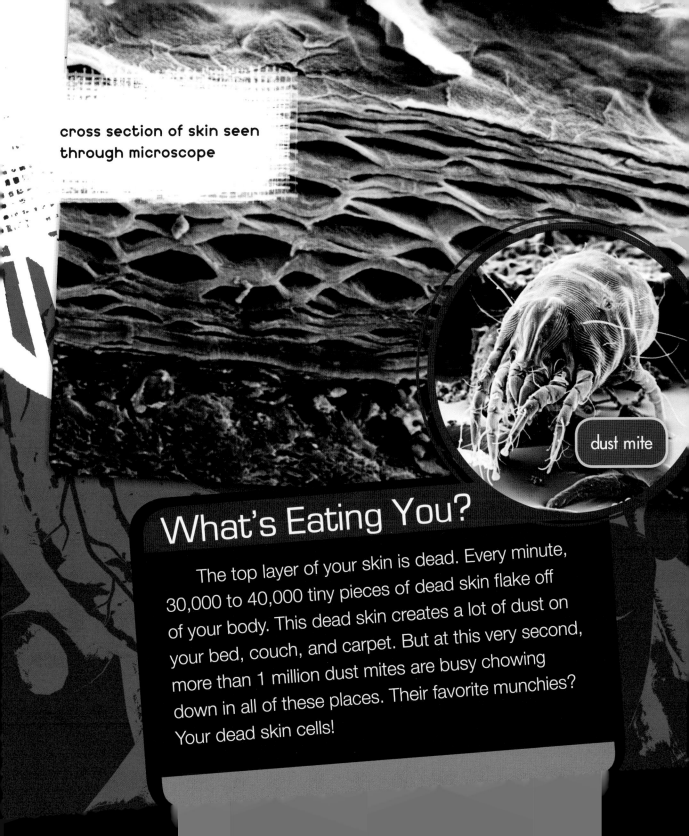

cross section of skin seen through microscope

dust mite

What's Eating You?

The top layer of your skin is dead. Every minute, 30,000 to 40,000 tiny pieces of dead skin flake off of your body. This dead skin creates a lot of dust on your bed, couch, and carpet. But at this very second, more than 1 million dust mites are busy chowing down in all of these places. Their favorite munchies? Your dead skin cells!

BODY FACT

More than 640 muscles in your body help you to move.

Under the Skin

If you could peel away your skin, you would find muscles underneath. Muscles are organs too. Some muscles, like your heart, are major organs that you need to live. Other muscles, like the ones in your arms and legs, help you move.

Some muscles help other organs do their jobs. The bladder is a muscle-lined pouch that stores urine until you go to the bathroom. Without the muscles surrounding your bladder, you would leak pee all over the place.

If you stripped away all your muscles, you would find your bones. Like muscles, bones are organs too. Together all of these bones make up the skeleton. Your skeleton supports your body and allows you to stand up and walk. Some of the large bones also have an important job. They make blood **cells** in their soft, spongy centers. The spongy center of a bone is called bone marrow.

cell — the smallest unit of a living thing

CHAPTER 2

Vital Organs

When most people think of organs, they picture the ones in the chest and **abdomen**. Hiding under your ribs, the lungs and heart are major organs you couldn't live without.

Take a Deep Breath

Your lungs are two squishy, pinkish organs that look like sponges. Breathe in. Can you feel your chest getting bigger? Your lungs have filled up like a balloon. When you breathe in, **oxygen** is brought into your body. Your body needs this oxygen to live.

You also use your lungs to talk. When you breathe out, air passes over your vocal cords. Air rushing over closed vocal cords makes sounds. Without lungs, you wouldn't be able to talk, sing, laugh, or live!

> **abdomen** — the part of the body between the chest and hips
> **oxygen** — a colorless gas that people need to breathe

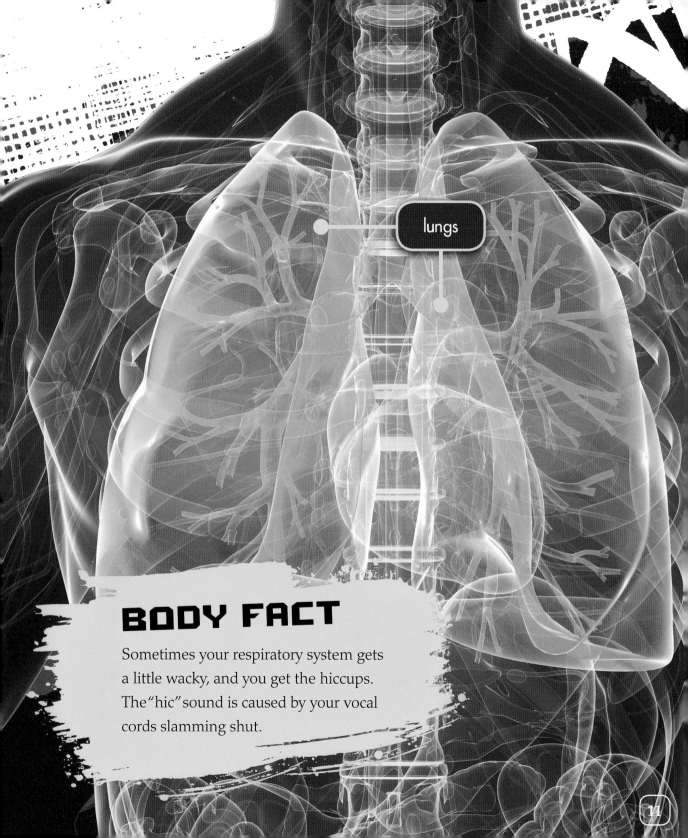

lungs

BODY FACT

Sometimes your respiratory system gets
a little wacky, and you get the hiccups.
The "hic" sound is caused by your vocal
cords slamming shut.

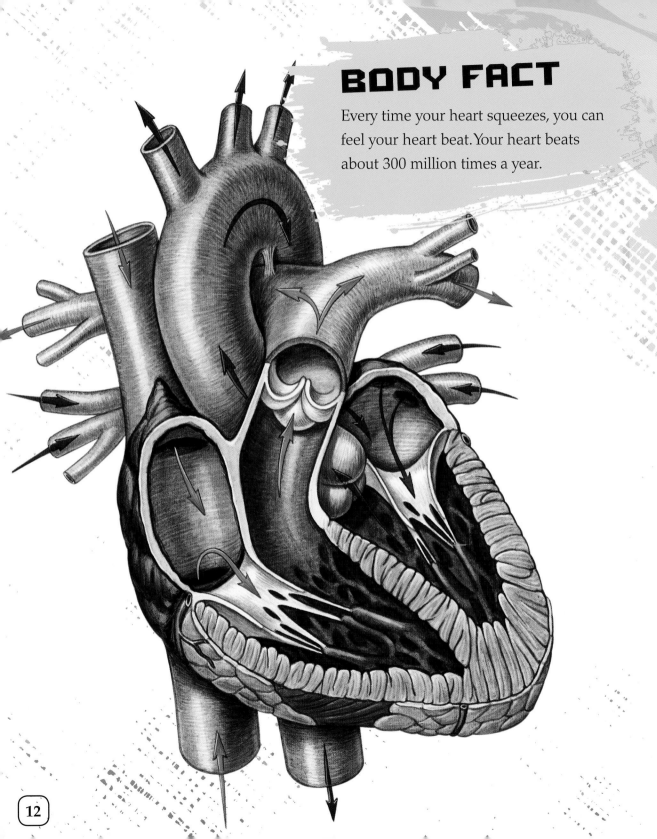

Feel the Beat

Your heart is safely nestled between your lungs. This important organ is about the size of your closed fist. But it doesn't look much like a Valentine's Day heart. Your heart actually looks like a pear.

Blood picks up oxygen as it flows through your lungs. Then it travels to the heart. When the left side is filled with blood, the heart squeezes tight like a fist. This squeeze squirts your blood though tiny tubes called blood vessels. The blood vessels carry blood and oxygen to the rest of your body.

All the cells in your body use oxygen from your blood. They replace the oxygen with **carbon dioxide**. Blood carrying carbon dioxide goes to the right side of your heart. From there, this blood is pumped to your lungs. Carbon dioxide leaves your body every time you breathe out.

> **carbon dioxide** — a colorless gas that people breathe out

The Liver Delivers

Like your heart and your lungs, the liver is an organ you couldn't live without. In fact, the liver is your largest internal organ. In adults, this wedge-shaped, spongy organ is about the size of a football.

The liver has many important jobs. Your liver makes a liquid called **bile** that breaks down the fat you eat. It also stores vitamins and energy that your body needs. But the liver's most important job is cleaning your blood.

bile — a green liquid that helps to digest food

BODY FACT

If your liver stopped working, you would die in about 24 hours. But even if 75 percent of your liver is removed, you would be able to survive.

liver

gallbladder

The Green Organ

Hidden under the liver is a small, pear-shaped organ called the gallbladder. This little organ isn't dark red, like you might expect. It's green! The color comes from the bile that the gallbladder holds. When you eat a large meal, your body needs more bile than your liver can supply all at once. The gallbladder stores extra bile to help digest those extra big meals.

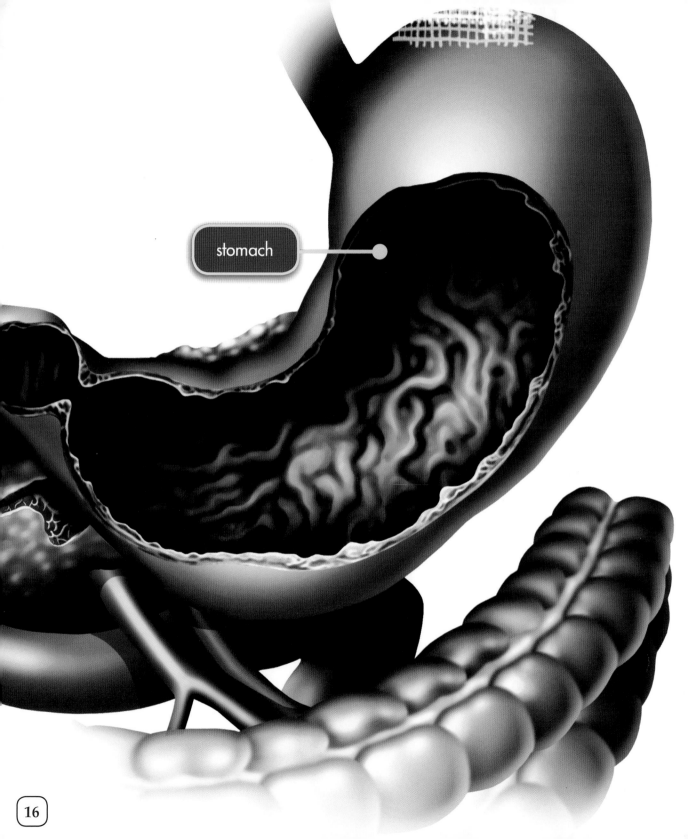

stomach

The Spleen

On your left side below your liver, you have a soft, purplish-red organ called the spleen. This fist-shaped organ is about the same size as your heart. The spleen **filters** your blood to get rid of germs. You could live without your spleen. But people who have had their spleens removed get sick more often.

The Growler

Like the spleen, the stomach lies just below the liver. You probably know a lot about your stomach already. It's the organ that growls when you are hungry. This stretchy, muscle-lined sack holds the food you eat. The stomach mixes food with digestive juices. These chemicals begin breaking down the food to release energy for the body.

> **filter** — to remove unwanted materials

CHAPTER 3

Movers and Shakers

Below your stomach lies an army of organs waiting to work. These organs each have a job to do before food leaves your body as waste. First the food goes to your small intestine, but not all at once. The muscle that separates the stomach and small intestine controls the amount of food leaving the stomach. This muscle allows only a little bit of food into the small intestine at a time.

BODY FACT

Digestion is a slow process. Food travels more than 20 feet (6 meters) through your body at about 1 inch (2.5 centimeters) per minute.

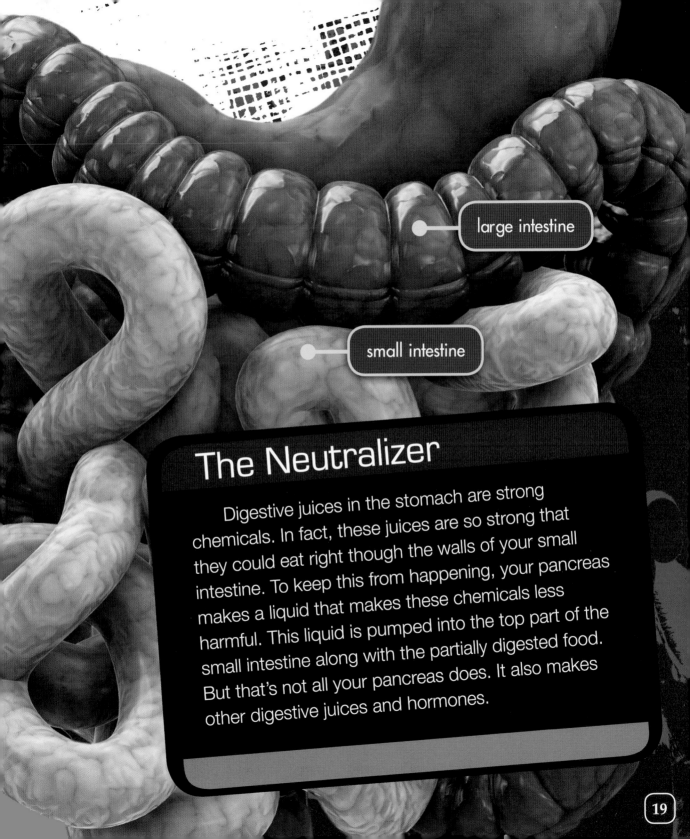

large intestine

small intestine

The Neutralizer

Digestive juices in the stomach are strong chemicals. In fact, these juices are so strong that they could eat right though the walls of your small intestine. To keep this from happening, your pancreas makes a liquid that makes these chemicals less harmful. This liquid is pumped into the top part of the small intestine along with the partially digested food. But that's not all your pancreas does. It also makes other digestive juices and hormones.

The Nutrient Taker

The small intestine is the longest organ in your body. This long, squiggly tube is only about 2 inches (5 centimeters) around. But it can stretch to about 20 feet (6 meters) long.

The small intestine breaks down food into **nutrients** that give your body energy. Tiny, fingerlike knobs called villi line the inside of the small intestine. These small pieces of tissue grab nutrients and pass them into your blood. By the time the food leaves your small intestine, all the nutrients have been sucked out.

nutrient — a substance needed by a living thing to stay healthy

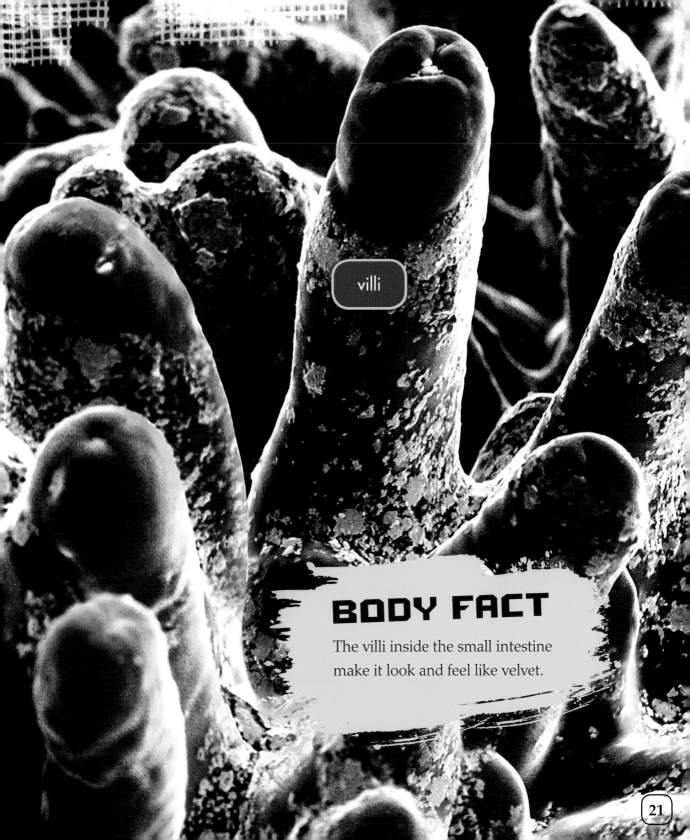

villi

BODY FACT

The villi inside the small intestine make it look and feel like velvet.

The Poop Maker

After the small intestine takes the nutrients from the food, only waste and water are left. But your body isn't done with it yet. The leftover food moves to the large intestine where it turns into poop. The large intestine removes most of the water for the body to use. As the water is removed, the waste gets packed tighter and becomes more solid. The lower part of the large intestine, called the rectum, stores the poop until you find a bathroom.

BODY FACT

The large intestine is only about 5 feet (1.5 meters) long. It's called the large intestine because it is wider than the small intestine.

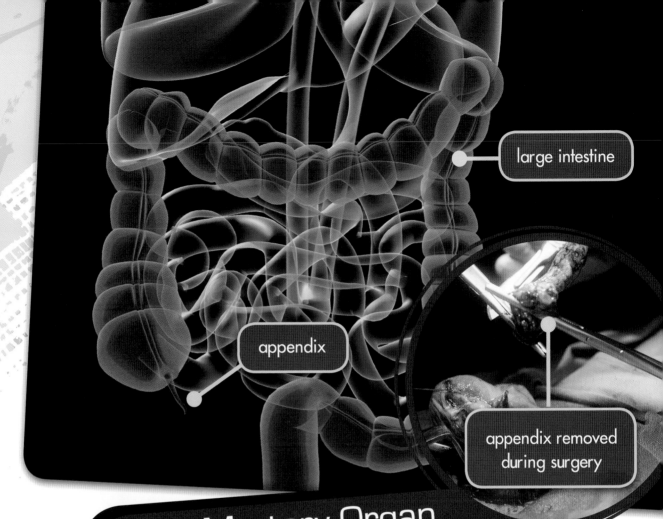

large intestine

appendix

appendix removed
during surgery

The Mystery Organ

The appendix is a tiny, fingerlike pouch attached
to the large intestine. Nobody knows what it does.
The appendix doesn't seem to have any job at all.
But if it gets infected, watch out! You become really
sick, really fast. And when it is infected, the appendix
hurts a lot. The only way to stop the pain is to have a
doctor remove your appendix.

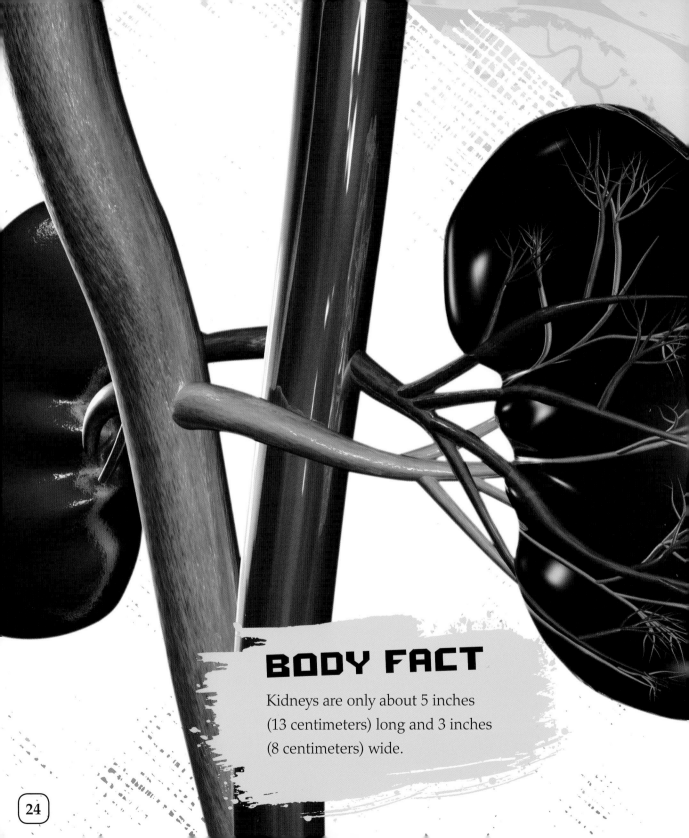

BODY FACT

Kidneys are only about 5 inches (13 centimeters) long and 3 inches (8 centimeters) wide.

Filter It Out

Two reddish-brown, bean-shaped kidneys hide behind your liver and stomach on either side of your backbone. Your kidneys help keep your blood clean. They filter blood to remove unwanted chemicals and extra water. Once the blood is cleaned, it continues on to other parts of your body. The waste chemicals and leftover water drain down small tubes into the bladder.

Gotta Go

The bladder is a stretchy, muscle-lined pouch in the lower part of your belly. Waste chemicals and water wait here until you use the bathroom. Together these chemicals and water are called urine. Your bladder can hold about 4 cups (1 liter) of urine. But your body tells you to start looking for a place to go when it is only half full.

Working Together

In order for you to stay healthy, your organs must all do their jobs. Your skin keeps your internal organs in place. Your lungs help you get oxygen. Your heart pumps blood from your lungs to other parts of your body.

Organs also must work together. The organs of your digestive system break down the food you eat. They work together to get nutrients from your food. Your large intestine, kidneys, and bladder get rid of waste. Your spleen gets rid of germs that could make you sick. Without organs, what would you do? Not much. Your organs do the hard work of keeping you alive.

BODY FACT

There are 10 major organ systems at work in your body.

Organs Diagram

A **Lungs** — Your lungs are not the same size. The left one is smaller than the right to leave room for your heart.

B **Heart** — An adult's heart pumps about 4,000 gallons (15,142 liters) of blood a day.

C **Liver** — If your liver is damaged, it can make new liver cells from healthy cells.

D **Stomach** — Food can stay in your stomach for three to four hours.

E **Small Intestine** — The small intestine is about as long as a school bus when stretched out.

F **Large Intestine** — The large intestine is also called the bowel.

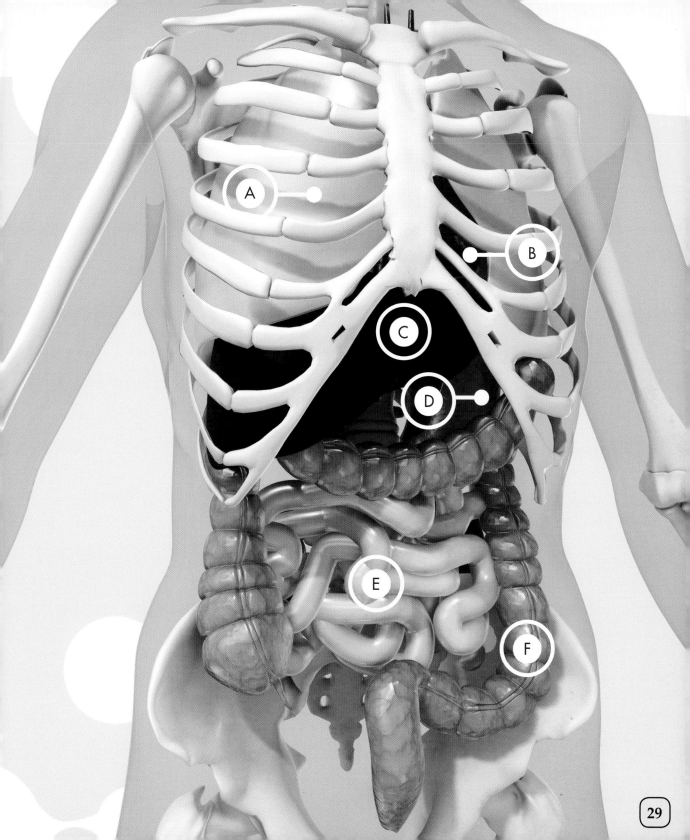

Glossary

abdomen (AB-duh-muhn) — the part of the body between the chest and hips

bile (BILE) — a green liquid that helps to digest food

carbon dioxide (KAR-buhn dye-OK-side) — a colorless gas that people breathe out

cell (SEL) — the smallest unit of a living thing

digestion (dye-JESS-chuhn) — the process of breaking down food so that it can be absorbed into the blood

filter (FIL-tur) — to remove unwanted materials

hormone (HOR-mohn) — a chemical made by the body that affects how a person grows and develops

internal (in-TUR-nuhl) — inside the body

nutrient (NOO-tree-uhnt) — a substance needed by a living thing to stay healthy

oxygen (OK-suh-juhn) — a colorless gas that people need to breathe

respiratory (RESS-pi-ruh-taw-ree) — related to the process of breathing

Read More

Katz Cooper, Sharon. *Major Organs: Sustaining Life*. Exploring Science. Minneapolis: Compass Point Books, 2007.

Parker, Nancy Winslow. *Organs!: How They Work, Fall Apart, and Can Be Replaced (Gasp!)*. New York: Greenwillow, 2009.

Spilsbury, Richard. *Cells, Tissues, and Organs*. The Human Machine. Chicago: Heinemann, 2008.

Internet Sites

FactHound offers a safe, fun way to find Internet sites related to this book. All of the sites on FactHound have been researched by our staff.

Here's all you do:

Visit *www.facthound.com*

FactHound will fetch the best sites for you!

Index